itch

poems
& prose

ZANE FREDERICK

central
avenue
PUBLISHING

2023

Published by Central Avenue Publishing, an imprint of Central Avenue Marketing Ltd.
www.centralavenuepublishing.com

itch,

Trade Paperback: 978-1-77168-280-0
EPUB: 978-1-77168-281-7

Published in Canada
Printed in United States of America

1. POETRY / General   2. POETRY / LGBT

10 9 8 7 6 5 4 3 2 1

Itch discusses topics regarding:

Self-loathing

Doubt

Longing

Ache

Hope

Anger

Forgiveness

Fear

Confidence

Contentment

AUTHOR'S NOTE

I've never been very good at introductions. I never know how to start things off or how to end them or leave them be. Poetry has been a mechanism for making sense of my memory and for healing it. For the past three years, I've been chewing on words that hurt to say. I've traced scars that demand attention I've neglected. Traumas I've ignored rather than process. Griefs I've refused to shed tears for. Anger boiling in me like a volcano overlooking a quiet town. This collection is the eruption. It's the hot, molten emotion overflowing.

I look at this book as a reflection of my early twenties. Here is where I learned how to document my nightmares. Where I wrote about longing for a love I never met. This is where I first wrote about the only boy who touched me like he owned me. It's where I questioned how I got here. How I became this matted mess. Why I turned out to be a wounded deer. I mistook old bruises for birthmarks, like they'd always been a part of me. I figured out where to bury the hurt and how to hold a grudge from a distance. I found myself in a limbo of forgiving and forgetting. I hope you find a way to make peace from these pages.

I caution you against taking advice from someone who falls in love with strangers, but I offer this: Give your pain permission to be felt. Be the captor of your ache. Grab it by the horns and ride it out. Pick the hell out of your scabs. Let them bleed. Let them sting. Learn to care for your sores.

The wounds that itch don't have to keep scratching us.

AT-SEA FEELINGS

I am a sailor of my emotions,
Which have trust issues with my gut.
Sticking my finger to the wind
So I may know which way is up.

I see it over there. Past the fog and mist.

The house with the light on the cliff,
Drawing the times I once cherished.

Can I distinguish
What matters to hold
From all these at-sea feelings
Just hoping to make it home?

I have written prologues in your honor,

But stories like ours aren't meant to have sequels.

SOUNDING OUT

I'm trying out the tones to know
How to express all my grief.
       It's fury,
Daybreak,
And the longing
In its teeth.

There's a pitch I've yet to find when
I'm screaming at the headlines on the news.
       Butting politics,
       Climate crisis,
       And the muse
       Who looks like you.

Though how do you name the strain
On heartstrings when the emotions pile up?
       I call out the doubt,
The desire, and
The feelings that
Have felt enough.

If nostalgia is a train,
Then I am lying on its tracks.

> *Found a bed in the vibrations*
> *And heard the calling of my past.*

WHEN THE EMPLOYER ASKS WHAT MY WEAKNESSES ARE

Still thinking you look good after a haircut.

Biting at the nerves under my nails.

Directing futures with people who don't know my name.

Reaching for small talk.

Walking out with half-baked goodbyes.

Looking back.

Going against the grain.

Being a sharp corner in an empty kitchen.

Stars exploding when I get too close.

Holding hands that don't hold back.

Taking too long to let go.

Missing the old you. / / Still missing the new one.

LONELY TWENTIES

The lonely twenties are roaring.
I flee from my busy reality,
Having the time of my life
Inside a fantasy.

I don't have it in me to love,
Because you know I'm a sucker for ruining things.
You tell me to come to the table,
But what would I bring?

OVERTIME

Where do I put this anxiety
When all it knows how to do
Is take up space?

How do I tell someone
About the heaviness without
It being too much to take?

Sometimes I turn into nightmares
And the fears I make up.
I don't want someone
To have to breathe for the both of us.

A24 REJECT

What if I am destined to be the desperate lead
Of a film no one wants to direct?
I think I'll always be a one-star review.
The box office butcher.
A foreign film never watched because
I can't be understood without subtitles.
Though I believe in redemption and
Happiness inside of endings.
I'll stay in suspense
For closure in the credits.

SHY

You caught me boarding the Brooklyn-bound train,
Playing piano in the air to Clairo's "Wade."
You keep looking at my chest
As if my heart is about to burst out of it.
I wonder if you're trying to guess my name.

I'll say it in a low tone so only you know.
If you start to ask about my life,
I apologize if I try to hide.
Tell me, what does my disguise
Look like in the light?

Does it look velvet soft, like a familiar face?
Or is it crimson, like the flags I wave?

CRASH SITE

I am a landing strip made of piano keys
And I like to think they all sound pretty,
But no impetuous pilots have planned
To come down on the tarmac of my terror.

Speaking from experience,
I am more crash site than soft ground,
And my body becomes an earthquake
As their wheels touch down.

THE THINGS I WOULD TELL MY THERAPIST IF I WASN'T AFRAID

I haven't made an appointment in months
Because I'm embarrassed by my burdens.
I don't know how to make them pretty
Without them hurting me.
And someone loves me, but I don't know
How to hold that in my hands. I was born
Clumsy and distracted. I know how to let go of things
Before holding on to them. I want to love beyond my capacity,
But I know it's safer to feel lonely
Than to show someone how to know me.

CRUMBS

Loneliness has never really moved out of me.
It's been the next-door neighbor
Who brings Bundt cakes and casseroles I don't want
But accept anyway.

I'm always hungry for a feeling.

CONVERSATIONS I NEED TO HAVE

The conversation where I tell my therapist exactly
Why I'm sitting in the chair.
The conversation where I draw all my scars in the sand
And watch the moon pull the tides over it.
The conversation where I cover all my fears:
Never to be heard out loud, never to be loved out in the open.
The conversation where I remember the light
Dimming from my eyes every day that summer
When I found out what he was doing in the dark.
The conversation where I confess how I almost kissed the boy
And had I done it, I'd be another strange face in his catalog.
The conversation where I hoard all the worst parts of me
Like I'm some fire hazard waiting to ignite.

These conversations are not pretty, but they are my naked faces;
They are raw and transparent. They are the kaleidoscope messes
That many have not looked through but have seen shimmer
Just a little.

TWENTY-SOMETHING HUGS LITTLE-BOY SELF

I stamp my scrapbooks
Of California summers and candid holidays,
Left with the red-eyed photos
Of all the troubles I made.

I developed the behaviors and patterns
That made me dance and play. Though
That little boy also needed to survive somehow,
So he learned how to stray.

> *Smoke lingered around my childhood.*
> *A reminder that it was warm*
> *Even when something was on fire.*

MOTHER'S GENES

My grandmother was a promising thing,
Always waiting for the crack of dawn. A night owl
With tired wings, finding a reason to laugh.
She was a soul of stories upon stories, never knowing
Which were real and which were made up.

My grandfather was a brick chimney.
All steady smoke, always letting off a little steam.
He was a writer too, held metaphors in his beer belly.
A soft bear of his own nature.

Together, they loved with a kind of recklessness, enough
To birth a daughter more put-together.
She came with fresh batteries and quick wit.
A true daddy's girl. A certain calm to her mother's storm.

CAREGIVERS

I'm learning that my superheroes have flaws.
They raised me to tape glass back together.
To sweep ash under the rug after they explode,
Restocking the house with peace and silver civility.
Give them a reason to remember that love can
Still exist between the cracks of the bad days.
And when the clouds move to
Different homes to rain on,
Love always knows how to come back
In the forecast.

HUMBLE ABODE

I hate that I house everyone else's emotions
When I barely make enough space for my own.
I've turned selfish with my solitude
And retire as the super they've known.

That doesn't mean I won't invite empathy
For tea when friends vent to me.
Though I've learned to set limits and boundaries.
Removed walls to feel more deeply.

LOUISE'S KNEES

When my grandmother hit the floor,
I heard the carpet calling me quick.
I could barely pick up the weight of her grief
When she shouted how sorry she was
For falling the way old people do,
Like a stiff avalanche slipping.
I lived in the silence she brought.
In the quiet intensities that kept one ear perked.
She made me afraid of midnights
And taught me how to live in the loudness
Of someone else's dependence.
She slept with her rosary that night for comfort,
And I hope the heaven she believed in
Caught her pleading knees.

LITTLE POSSESSIONS

What is with these familiar ghosts?
They float along the balcony where
My thoughts watch the stars count each other.
What do they want in a place I already haunt?
I'm sure there are vices to fight and faces to face
And apparitions of my favorite soul
I still see in a crowded place.

Have my demons come to claim
All the crimes they committed?
Did they come to scratch my scars?
Line my skin like reminders of what I have not forgiven.

Tiny canyons of grief. I hike them anyway.

Even all the friends I made
after you know your name.
I didn't think your memory
would last this long.

USE ME

The boy that turned me into a writer
Now shows love to my poems in the way
I wish he'd show love to me.

>Studying me carefully, never to
>Put me down, even when he's finished.
>I could have been his bestseller.
>His bedside read.
>His nightstand man.
>Whatever he wanted me to be.

MALIBU

I'm sure there are other lovely shores
To rest my lonely ships on, but
I only want to land on yours.

Oh, beautiful beach,
Won't you harbor me?

THIS IS HOW IT STARTS

I'm already writing poems about you,
And I don't even know your favorite color.

I'd cross state lines to get to know you
And be your end-of-summer lover.

Could our timing one day be right,
If at this moment it isn't yet?

Am I allowed to miss someone
I haven't even met?

ATOMS

I dress down my pursuit so it doesn't
Look like I'm the stalking kind.

I wait for my cue to carry you out
Like some perfect crime.

I won't dare to hunt you down, honey.
You are not mine to find.

Do I sound sincere when I apologize for the way
All my atoms try to love you at the same time?

THEFT

You said you would be on your way
Once October came, but now it's passing by.
If only I could come to conclusions sooner.

Because even though I want it to,
I know that it won't be you,

So why the hell am I
Still forcing futures?

WEATHER VANE

We wake in the space between
What could have been,
And in cities that are not our hometown,
Wondering what ever happened.

Perhaps I got caught up in your wind,
My finger becoming a weather vane,
So desperate to follow you, to hear
Your tongue buzz my name.

And I could ask if you're still coming
Or I could stop waiting for a call.
I thought maybe when you met me
You would forget about Utah.

You have always been a cowboy on the move,
But if you ever change your mind,
I would leave Phoenix behind.

YOU'RE LIVING RENT-FREE UP IN MY DREAMS
BUT IN THE MORNING, YOU STILL AREN'T MINE.
IF WE'RE NOT GOLDEN UNTIL WE FALL ASLEEP,
WILL YOU WAKE ME WHEN YOU GIVE US A TRY?

I'LL BUZZ YOU UP

Tell me if you want to move in or move on.

We could grow small and live
In a tiny Christmas village.
Like the ones in the mall.

Quaint and vibrant. Frozen inside
A ceramic mold of what could
Be a love that thaws.

We both know snow, and it's
Getting colder here in New York.
Meet me on my front stoop
Or call me toward Park City. I'll lie
By your mountainside anytime.
And you're always welcome to
Sit by my stairwell in hell.

BABY IN THE BACK SEAT

I miss the you I've been missing out on.

Looking west toward the mountains you sit by, screaming,

You're so cool!

And you are. You're cocky and you know it, but you're a sweet tooth.

I only hope to find the kind of love I keep writing about losing.

But there should be a warrant out for my wanting.

The way it stalks just to keep up.

How it writes fiction in the name you called me: King.

But am I? I wear a cowardly crown, but I could butter up my brain.

Change the routes to avoid spiral.

I'm a virgin to really holding a heart that beats fine in my hands.

Wouldn't it be a pleasure to be loved by a prototype?

I could say it's your loss but it doesn't have to be.

I'll be your baby in the back seat if you let me.

HAIL ME DOWN

Where are you off to next, sweet boy?
Another beach in Malibu
Or a neighboring town you've never been to?
I'm on the Upper East Side,
Finding your face in strangers
Who are just look-alikes.
You must be having trouble finding me.
Here, I'll call you. Do you see?
I'm in the green striped shirt in Yorkville,
Waiting for you, still.

Waving like you're a taxi coming back for me.

But what if when you reach for me
you won't like what you're holding on to?

SAINT

You don't know I miss
Your holiday pics.
I keep a tab open or two.

You promised me
You'd visit my city
But April went, then May and June.

So why don't you go
Back to the North Pole
Where I still believe in you.

MALADAPTIVE DAYDREAMING

I speak of you like we live in the same home,
Your name ingrained in my brain,
But your number does not live in my phone.
Who is it I'm talking to in my passenger seat?
What is it I try to recall when I wake from a dream?

I'm curious to know you. I would study in the park where I lie,
Take notes and listen close like you're a podcast I play.
I would pull an all-nighter just to memorize your face.
To learn about your past and the moons around your wounds.
I can tell you have been injured before.
I'll show you mine if you show me yours.

      I think you might bring out the best in me.
      I'll show you yours if you show me mine.

ARIES ANGEL

Happy belated birthday. I curse my growth for forgetting.
Catch me up to speed, cowboy.
Tell me, how was Seattle? The market looked grand, and you did too.
Pike Place got to see your face and I'm jealous as hell. Tell me,
How many ungrateful strangers got a glimpse without a double take?
For you I would do a thousand, turn into the owl who prowls.

Oh yeah! How was it in Arizona?
You were there too, mapped in gold.
 (I'm sorry for keeping tabs on you that I never plan to close.)
Was it as hot as you recalled?
Did it feel worse knowing I was a highway away?

 I hope to remain a right turn missed.
 A street you always look down.
 Short-term memories with not enough nostalgia.
  I wish you reached for more.
 I am an update in your refresh, moving
 Further from you, and you don't even flinch.
 I worry you might make me forget how to write about wanting.

Tell me if peace ever comes after a treaty of trying.

I don't think it does.

ODE TO THE CAR YOU WOULD'VE USED TO COME SEE ME

There are dozens of gas stations
On the stretch between us
And if you turn around now,
You might catch the sundown
And have time to forget who
You said you were on your way for.

With me it's always going to be out of the way.
You don't have to keep the seat warm on the passenger side.
Save your brakes for something worth stopping for.
I promise I'm not worth the drive,

JEROME

You were the one to learn my name first.
You found me out of the blue.
If you didn't want me then, babe,
Then what's the point of wanting you?

Because our love's a ghost still haunting this town,
And we're the tourists hunting them down.

But I find it tiring to beg for residing.
I won't let this be where I retire.
I'll grow clever and know better
When my hair grays and conscience sways
To this place we once admired.

HORCRUX

Where are the remnants of your leaving?
I have been digging through my pockets,
Under mattresses and couch cushions,
Between car seats and memories.
I don't know how much more of you
Is left to let go of until you are
Really gone from my grasp.

I've loosened my grip
But you're still at my fingertips.

*I'm not sure how
to let go of things
that I think would
be good for me.*

AFTERLIFE

I wouldn't keep running toward the cemetery
If I didn't feel like there was a part of us
Still buried alive.

Tell me you feel the gravesite uprooting.
You must admit there is life
Somewhere we aren't.

> You used to call the shots;
> Now you don't even call.

But you could still be my midnight prank.
Just aim and shoot, and I'll follow
The flare back to you.

HOARDER

You break into all my dreams
Without invite and yet I still
Make a plate for you at the table.
Pour you a drink at my parties.
Make room in my heart when all
That extra space used to be filled
To keep you out.

BLIZZARD

If you're feeling lonely,
Just look northeast.
My love lingers like
A foggy morning
After a busy storm.
It may not be a love
You want, but it's
A love that will die
Wanting you.

BLUEBERRY STAIN

How easy was it for you to forget me?
To clear me from your frontal lobe
And turn me into a stranger
You never really got to know.

You have become a blueberry stain
On my brain, candied and tempting.
I can't tell if you are poison or a sweet thing.
But I will still die satisfied at having
The chance to want you this long,
Even without your blessing.

BLIND SPOT

I'm somewhere behind you now,
When I used to be your forethought.

And when you took back all your sparks,
Was I something you forgot?

No matter your answer,
I hope you don't mind me
Forever cruising,
Trying to start fires
In your blind spot.

HUM

If not you then tell me who
Would be worth the wait?
No other patience
Would ever
Equate.

MY LOVE LANGUAGE MUST BE:

Terrorizing.

Loving from horizonless distances.

Counting the words in our small talk.

Accepting crumbs.

Asking for more.

Still calling it love.

Bracing for impact.

Always having my blinker on.

Never turning.

Running red lights.

Playing it cool.

Using teeth.

Saving you a seat.

Being the mess I promised I would be.

BAD TIMING

Did I leave the note too close to the edge?
My number falling past the palms I'll never hold.
Will my misguided call be another
Misfit shipped out to that lonely island?
A sweet story never to be told.

THERAPY NOTES

My sister says

> *You need a love that's easy.*

Love has never been easy for me,
But maybe I just make it hard
For myself.

ACHILLES

I've been in love with ideas,
Beautiful apparitions of
My greatest infatuations,
But never something genuine.
I've imagined the prettiest shapes.
Color palettes that match my life.
But it is all mundane.
I've pined for technicolor realities
That were just distant daydreams
When zoomed out.
I'm a fool to think I could
Be loved from up close.
I push and I push and I push.
My lungs have adopted a third
From how often I run.
You would think I'm always
Being held captive by the
Same hands that only want
To hold my roughest limbs.
I think I could be made soft if I really let him.

It's like I survive on escape
And yet in a cruel way,
I prepare my Achilles
For the next chase.

Why do I fault love as if it owes me
something I have never found.

You were never mine to figure out.

WARNING

I will reach for your hand
Before you know how
To pronounce my last name.
I will point out all the exit signs
And warning labels.
I can't promise I will be
Something safe, so just
Let me know if I am
Getting too close and if
You plan to escape.
I'll even leave the window open
The night you sneak out
And when I wake to the curtains
Flowing, I'll know you made it out.
As you find your way back to
The spot before we began,
Ask my next love how much
They'll bargain for.
Ask if they're okay with
Carrying handfuls.
Tell them about how much
I'll love the space they take.

i set myself
up for heartbreak
like placing bear traps
in my forests trying
to tame all my

wild loneliness

GROWING UP

I grew tall when the hurt stretched farther than the growing pains.
You could hear me screaming for miles.
I got my first paycheck at eighteen
Though I didn't know who
I was until I was twenty-two, looking back
At all the wreckage I walked through.
I grew tall when my first love started
Feeling like an exit ramp coming up on the doomed
Highway I had been cruising for too long.
I grew even taller when I found out
My parents were human. No longer superheroes.
No fancy cape and funny face, just sorrow and
Different versions of *I'm sorry.*
I'm a grown-up with dog days and
My own version of downward spiral.
I'm a selfish city that takes
And takes and takes.

FLINGS & FLEETINGS

I've only ever known flings and fleetings,
Forever finding routes to take that will keep me safe
From maintaining a feeling.

I'm still learning how to love accessible people.
No longer the idea of these faces that look
Like love if I stand back far enough.
Only a few brave names have been
Damned to love me to some capacity.
Saw a heaven in me that I've never found.
So if you're looking for peace,
Go scour the beach. I'm in the city,
Wreaking havoc on the hearts
I'll never learn how to keep.

OFFSPRING OF ICARUS

I back out of my tattoo appointment last minute.
My forearm sighs. Empty.
Maybe I didn't spend enough time wanting it.
I try to be better at hanging around.
At following through.
At following in general.
I don't think I was born a flight risk
But I always seem to retreat
From the potential of permanence.

What kind of lover does that make me?

Does my loyalty rust the more demanding
It becomes? Am I the offspring of Icarus
When I get too close to the sun?

IMPOSSIBLE!

To teach new tongues how to love me
Is to send astronauts to the sun.
It's to burn more intensely
Than anything you've known.
And I apologize in advance
If you don't make it out
With your steady, soft hands.

To love me is to learn the impossible.

LATE BLOOMER

Wandering through life,
I've always had myself,
But lately my lonely wonders
What it'd be like with someone else.

I think the part of me that longs
Is young and still afraid of change,
But what if being a lover
Is not part of my DNA?

ESTRANGED

I've only ever known the me I go home to at night.
I haven't met the one who lies in the bends of your limbs.
I've heard of changing for the better, but I'm not sure if you
Would've been the seedling of my love or just another setting sun.
There must be an answer in your absence.
I was a thesaurus of the things I was afraid to become,
And now I search synonyms for martyr.
I won't admit that I almost died to want you.
But hell, I'll let this longing linger at my wake.
I'll hear your footsteps in the grass.
Say you'll leave dandelions on my grave.

You come back
around like
the seasons that
get me down

KENNEDY'S HOUSE

I'm at this party and pray you don't show.
I can't bear to see the ghost
Of the one I've missed the most.
The one who won't need tippy-toes
To reach my highest hopes.

And if I see you at this party,
I'm afraid my what-ifs will scream
In the houses you used to haunt.
The ones I trained myself
To forget how to want.

And if I see you at this party,
Will my old wounds sting
From all your sweet nothings?
Will you look at me like
We could've been something?

PERPENDICULAR

If you listen closely, those old sirens
Of ours are sounding again.

I could have sworn they lost their voice
When I lost you.

What's left of the moon is spilling
Into this living room,
And we are cutting birthday cake
Like the tension we have been baking
For four summers now.

Somehow our last goodbye warped
Back into meeting all over again.

We touch gently when we leave,
Dispersing back into our busy, divided lives.

I like this perpendicular version of us.
Always running back into each other.

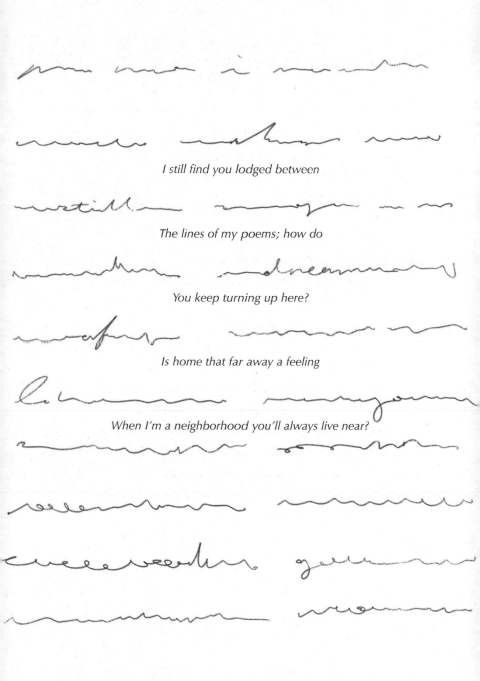

I still find you lodged between

The lines of my poems; how do

You keep turning up here?

Is home that far away a feeling

When I'm a neighborhood you'll always live near?

DREAMING TREE CABERNET

I recycled the wine bottle.

Five miraculous years escaping you and

I still have the cabernet you gave me for Christmas.

I drank it all by myself just before New Year's;

You should have seen it.

I kept the bottle, but you don't know that.

Left it on the desk of my last two apartments.

Full of flowers and unfinished metaphors about being drunk.

I gave an empty memory life again.

I'm moving back to New York on Saturday, and you said

Congrats on the job!!

I felt goosebumps raise their guard; my body forgot what it's like

For you to be proud of me. I've been stretching a suitcase, packing.

I've been making sacrifices and memorizing different goodbyes

For different people. There is no space for it on my flight

To a new life. But I'm giving up these tiny wonders.

I'm sure there are slivers of you in the wrinkles of my wardrobe

And the poems I'll never finish.

PAST DUE

I carved a library out of him, all for him.
Became a landmark of my longing.
I watched dust collect in the places
We used to touch. I kept track of
How many days ticked by since
The last time he read me out loud.
But in my hours alone, when my
Favorite recollections of us are past due,
I still wish it were him at the end
Of my aisles.

WHEN THE WRITER FALLS

Tell me what brave hands will
Uphold the position of writing
About you.

I am both the day shift and
The night auditor, the overworked
And underpaid, but it's the job
I signed up for when those
Baby blues came my way.

Your unrequitedness is
Immortalized in the words I write,
And all this longing has only ever
Belonged to you.

Who else will you cut so deep they bleed ink?

I HAVE BEEN:

◊   The flustered host

◊   The beggar

◊   Your suppressed secret

◊   The virgin heart dressed in white

◊   The nightmare

◊   The only real thing you can think of
                 When you think about love

◊   The one who stayed

◊   The one still holding your spot in line

I HAVE LIVED A MILLION LITTLE LIVES

WANTING YOU

INSIDE JOKES

You live inside the jokes
Between my friends and me.
A laugh that's easy to choke on
But a lie that always
Hurts to swallow.

I would love you with
My outside voice again
If I didn't oversaturate
The storyline. Retold
Far too many times to
Have extra pages for
A happy ending.
We read like boring history.
A tale so forgotten
Not even the survivors
Could recall the details.

YOU TOOK CARE OF ME

I'm reaching out because you're the only thing
I know how to hold on to.
The sun has gotten smaller since I left,
And now I know dark the way I used to know you.
My parents finally sold the old house.
I'm only saying that because I miss you
In the way I miss my childhood.
I mean I miss you in the way of things I know I can't get back.
I'm trying to break the fever dream I caught.
Would you nurse me back to health?
If I rate the pain, would it help you take it away?

YOUR MOVE

You moved out of your parents' house,
But I still wonder about your mother
And if she also thinks it's cruel
That we aren't with each other.
She never questioned how we mingled.
Watched us as if we'd moved like this before.
            (At least someone noticed.)
She smiled fondly when you introduced me.
You were slipping on the cliffside
And I watched you catch yourself.
I'm down here on the beach, baby.
The sand is soft and so are you.
Come pick pearls with me.
Put your fingers through my hair again,
Tug a little if you want. I miss the way
You domesticate and that look on your face.
Tell me which of my moves meant something to you.
Tell me to make another.

PRETTY PLEASE

If there was something to believe in
I would make a bed out of an altar.
I would fall to my knees and make
My please the prettiest one.
I won't beg for your return,
But I'll craft a wish on every
Star that has held on.

BRIM

Memory lane has become a dead-end street.
There are house fires where there used to be
Headlights in the driveway.
Traditions and celebrations.
Warm October dusks
Suspended in the air.

I'm not sure which rooms
To store our cache in anymore.

But I do know you were
The brim I once loved to.
And there will always be
Space for our memories to take.

WARRANTY

I'm trying hard to sit pretty in my present,
But you're a commercial break on loop.
I'm never not reminded of what is not mine.

Is there a way to move on
Without stringing you along?
Can I cut ties
Without saying goodbye?

YOU & ME IN TEMPE

We only talk every full moon or every time I find an excuse,
But I still hope life is being kind to you.

Sometimes I miss how you used to look at me,
Like some shooting star landing right on your front porch.

I think there are tire marks on the street where I dropped you off.
I think there are holes in the floor from where I wanted to kiss you.

I forgot to tell you, but I ran into your parents at a birthday party.
Your mom said she would say hi to you for me. I never asked her to.
I wonder if she really did. I think about your reaction.

I never thanked you for not feeling the same way,
And even though hearing your name still hurts an old version of me,
I can say it out loud now without feeling lonely.

Yours but never mine,
— Me

Every version of me will always long for any version of you.

ILY

You send me comic strips on the internet.
Years later. They're funny; so is this.
We found an opening in the closure.
A heartbeat in mourning.
My love language remains in our conversations.
In another dimension, we run into each other at the market.
Everything is fresh and locally grown; so are we.

CABLE KNIT

I study the creases I've made on my body.

All the parts of me that are wrinkled and not yet pressed.

No one has worn me (yet, I hope).

Though I was made to be worn out.

I used to let the roughest, most closed fists

Stretch my stitches and loosen my wounds.

But I do not belong in drawers nor corners.

Hang me around your neck like a collar you fix

Or your favorite cable knit.

There is still a light under the door
we closed years ago.

One of us must keep changing the locks and bulbs.

One of us must keep checking the peephole.

YOUR BIRTHDAY, 2021

Anger is the beast that lives in my basement.
It's what makes me a hoarder for the grudges that lose their color.
Lifeless bitterness I keep stored.

Anger is a red door with a scalding-hot knob.
It rattles and whistles. I don't know how to
Open it without setting off the alarms.

Anger is the knife that continues to twist in the sides you held,
In the back you caressed, and in the heart you could have owned.
You will always be a knock on my door.
You will always wake the beast.

QUARANTINE BLUE

You don't deserve a seat
At the table in my dreams.

I promised I wouldn't write
Another poem about you.

You don't deserve my words
When you have already taken
Almost everything else.

I hope you're bored as hell.

"FORGIVENESS" BY PARAMORE PLAYS

I would never wish you death,
But some days I dream about
How life would be if we
Had never met.

I would never wish you pain,
But sometimes I wonder
How my heart might
Have healed if you'd
Never cursed my name.

THE BARNES & NOBLE BY YOUR HOUSE

I haunt the bookstores you shop now that I hang in the aisles you
Walk.

A reminder of the writer who never wrote about you, but here we are.

Do you like the poems you pull out of me? Fingers that meet keys as
They bleed

Truths and melodramatics. It's the only place I talk to you still, and I
Don't like

Getting the last word anymore. But you had it first, babe, I read it.
Did you manage

To take anything else with you before I left? What about the fucks I
Handmade you?

Or did you leave them in a memory I cannot return to?

I'll learn forgiveness before a new synonym to describe my ache.

I owe it to my hands, which are used to your name as the subject.

I promise for pardon in the next poems I write.

I wonder if you think I stopped writing about you.
I'm curious if you wish I still do.
(And I do.)

SWALLOW

You cause all my undoings,
The mess on my chest
And all other things
My pride won't confess.
The moon has heard my cries
Far too many times for you
To keep me intertwined in
The confines of the cravings
You betray in my mind.

My hand remains victim
To the final blow that
You'll never know
You strike.

ONE YEAR LATER

Our leftover sparks started fires
That we keep spreading around.
We share this devastation the way
We used to share secrets, but you
Can have it all now.

I can't keep laying ashes to rest
When all they do is cloud my judgment,
So I reach for the hand of my mistake,
Extinguishing the place where our love met.

DITCH

December thawed the hands I held your cheeks with.

Mary Jane in our veins, I found the courage to lean in first.

My flag white and yours red, too close for comfort.

I should have known it then.

I let you coast across my skin like a highway never driven.

It was new and cool and it felt electric. You had your top down, babe,

There was music and wind; we could feel it.

So why did you freeze the trust given?

You slashed the tires of the one who gave you a ride.

Watched me skid across your skin,

And now I'm lying in the middle of that highway.

The exit signs look like your gestures.

Will I ever find the map to show

Which direction leads me back to my body?

HEAL IN HELL

I know you keep rewriting apologies
In ink that pleads and prays,
While you condemn your admittance
To the bed where we once lay.

I bet the ego you used against my body
Is now cologned in all your shame,
And if your stretched-out stitches ever heal,
I hope the scars spell out my name.

APOLOGIES IN THE MORGUE

I picture you a cadaver.
Cold and that same bitter grin.
I picture myself the pathologist.
The one with the blade again.
Forgiving you in a silence
That blares in my mind.

I examine your grinding teeth
Like a dentist looking for corrections.
I check under your fingernails to
See if my skin is still there.

The lifeless part of you that lies in front of me
Is just a sliver of who you used to be. Maybe.
You once slaughtered my innocence
When you were young and filled with spite.
I'm still learning how to find peace in my grief,
Knowing I gave you the knife.

SHARK

You said my mother never taught me depth,

Yet yours only loved you on the surface.

They say opposites attract but do they ever attack?

I would war-cry my way to your downfall.

I know the highways would be packed.

Do you hear the crowds? Do you hear their horns?

Their fingers point toward your gravesite.

I'll smile big so you can see how sharp my teeth got.

You once told all my friends about my bite,

So I'll open wide, in case you forgot.

GRUDGE

I bought new furniture and wall decor. I invested in my room,
Yet I stay living in the heat of the moment. We're tossing this
Smoke detector back and forth, and my body is tired of
Escaping in time. My wrist hurts from banishing you.
How dare you try breaking into my most intimate thoughts,
Never to give a damn. Your selfish attempts to notice
My daydreams, ask what I'm thinking about.
It's not you. And if it ever is, it's my beautiful escape.
Or it's the nightmares I shove behind my closet doors.
Chains won't fit and I've already tried that old chair trick,
So I'm stuck here with my back against it. Holding you up
And away from hurting me. From falling right back on top
Of me. The winters get colder and you are the cause of it.
I can handle the snow but when the officer pulls me over
Because of my windshield crack from our brittle past,
He too will know.
I'm still learning how to be okay with writing you like this.
I was never going to write you with love,
But if I ever did write,
Never did I think it would be with a grudge.

YOUR VICTIM

I press you hard against the wall, and you press against my wounds.

That's how I knew we were opposites. We attract,

But I taste blood when I kiss you.

I can't tell if it's yours or mine.

Maybe we'll end up on one of those murder documentaries.

You always did want to make a name for yourself. So make it.

Carve it into my chest. Lodge it between the eyes

You once looked into softly.

Show me the guts you told me about. Be a dear

And freshen me up before they find me here.

Place flowers around my head. Make it look like you honored

Me. Like you were setting me free. Look, I'm setting you free.

You dance off the hook. You still look for me in your dreams.

TRY AS YOU MIGHT

I didn't need the last word
To walk out knowing I blew up
Bridges with these hands.

You will never remember
How to cross me.

And I made sure your last memory of me
Was only the echoed footsteps
Of my leaving.

My name will always be a siren
You move out of the way for.

IS THERE A MEMORIAL TO HOLD?

We have had battles before, sweetheart.
Loud, violent hills and blue bubbles typing
I found craters in the city we used to maneuver.
I saw holes in the wall where I hung the painting you gave me.
I used to count the death toll but I lost track.
Don't tell me about the dead dreams. They were night terrors
And you made them pretty. I've given too many moments of silence.
I would pay my respects if I could afford them.

ARMY

If you just show me where you hid all my clumsy confessions,
I'll take them back. I'll take them all back. The ones cluttered
Under your bed and in between the in-betweens.
I want my love back. I want the gas mileage and cavities.
I want the apology from the old me.
I'll send a search party. I'll send the masses.
We're coming with flowers and threats.
We're not leaving without the rest.

FAREWELL

I never found the fair in my farewell, but I'll attempt it here.
I watched forgiveness seep into the dreams you sneak into,
But I'm not ready to spare you the mercy I've been making.
As the sun keeps wrapping itself around my days, I start to forget
Your freckles like you forgot my worth. I learned to melt the keys
That once let us in and craft closure like a blacksmith, and now
There are swords in every corner of me. I was always defenseless
In your tower, but I jumped out the window and freedom broke
My fall. I could wonder how you're doing now that my compliance
No longer revolves around your tricks, but instead I just cheer
For the quietude. My new life knows peace now that you aren't
Holding me captive.

I'M THE CLIMAX AND CLOSER

I'm a backlog of things left unsaid
So I'll declutter here: I hope I didn't
Imprint on your poems. You don't deserve
To try and write me in pretentious words
And cheap metaphors, but maybe I'll linger
In your hooks and closing lines.
It's a pleasure to know I'll always
Be something you lost.
Something you'll always
Write an ending to.

GRANNY SMITH

The orchard is not poisoned. No, you are just a bad apple.
You garden worm. My Granny Smith. So crisp with your wit
But no longer lingering in the grocery stores I shop in.
My summertimes will not spoil again even if my winters remember.

> I lost my appetite for the first half of healing,
> But I know there will be sweet Galas for me.
> And when I brave the farmer's market,
> I will visit the best stands. Search for
> The freshest kind of tender and
> Never mind the sour.

> I'll show up for me
> And it will taste like Liberty.

TAKE CARE

There were seasons I believed you could cradle my peace,
But it always hollered when you held me.
My skin blistered like you were sun poisoning,
Too much of a good thing.

There are still photographs of the rosacea cheeks you
Left me. My teenage years matured into the calmest blue,
But you lived in the only sky of mine where I would
Realign the moon, so you went and took my pretty blues.

You told me to take care, and you took that too.

Note to self: Promise you will find solace in the places
                they did not bruise.

DIRECTOR'S CUT

After you grow older
And get closer to the new friends you meet,
I hope you speak highly of me.

Don't tell them about the fires
That started when you heard me leave.

But if you tell them the tale,
Don't tell them the director's cut.
Speak about the truths
That are hard for you to keep.

Tell them about the quiet bruises.
How easy it was to rehearse your speech.

I wish you golf claps, but never standing ovations.
I dream you forgiveness, but never rest from remorse.

YELLOW CAKE

I'll bake closure out of new Junes and Julys
And freshly picked clementines.

I'll mix it in all the songs you ruined for me,
Knowing I danced you out in the kitchen until
I could really feel those songs again.

I won't take closure out of the oven burnt
With the absence of your apology anymore.

I'll let it cool by the window,
Let the hurt continue to heal and
Feel the scent of brand-news
Waft under my nose.

I bet you can smell me forgetting you.

I THOUGHT YOU WOULD GROW OUT OF IT
BY NOW

You keep making a path out of pathetic.

Cursing my name just for something to blame.

Look at all the acres you could use to grow, yet you

Choose to wilt in what hurt you years ago. And I

Hear you scream at the sky instead of looking inside.

Twenty-four and still keeping score.

I think that you'll be free of your crimes

Once you stop accusing me they're mine.

Break a leg, old friend.

*I'm still airing out absences
I shouldn't have made myself
hold on to.*

ITCH

My memory is sharp and elastic.
It latches onto every daydream
Summoned by the devil that guided
My shoulder right underneath your head.
And you nestled in my corners like
A houseplant. Or laundry tired of being worn.
Did I wear you out, babe? Were you a ball gown
At a block party? Did you find a way to
Fit up my sleeves and pull out all the tricks
I kept in secret? I was waiting patiently
Before you got comfortable kicking
Your shoes off in the foyer of my heart.
This is no place for mud and grime
On the feet you march over me.
I ache to forget the thorns I still feel poking
Around the places you once touched.
A bustling dining room now a place
Where loneliness is never really full.
It's a place I still itch. A place I feel always
Needs to be cleared from the table.

My life is better without
you demolishing it
but that doesn't mean
I don't miss the **wreckage** sometimes

ADDRESSED TO MYSELF

You don't hate the idea of love, you're just afraid
Of what it will look like in your hands.
You're so used to vacancy and space.
Beautiful solitude on do not disturb.
You have only been on a honeymoon once,
But maybe it was wrapped in sticky-note nostalgia
And stories from a storage shed.

You used to be so restless with the only heart you have,
Chasing after cowboys under the valley moon.
You never got the chance to be haunted by settling down.
            I hope your jinxes catch up to you.
            I hope you learn to pray for possession.
            I hope the longing lingers
But never strings you along like the one who peaked at the prom,
Desperate to have something worth looking back on.
I hope you know you are worth looking back on.

V CARD

My body knows of its virginity
And when the jokes were made,
They sounded like a time of death.
Like something to mourn.
But still being brand-new does not
Mean I have not been picked up.

I am not an open house for people
To walk in and out of before they invest.
I am also not the sad one for sale
On a cul-de-sac just because I have not let
Anyone in through the back door yet.

just because some parts
of me are damaged goods
does not mean they are
not still salvageable

DRAFT OF UNFINISHINGS

I let my hair grow out so I can learn how to braid it.

I let my flowers die so I can dig up the garden and build a shed.

    Inside, I put one bed, a lamp, and some plants, and I breathe

    A little more easily.

I become the distance between me and my old friends;

I still care for them out there.

I keep on making plans with myself. I never get tired of me.

I am a draft of unfinishings.

    A pile of redos and coming-soons,

    I'm turning out to be

    My favorite project.

I know I'm worthy of good love
but am I capable enough
to let myself receive it?

STRAWBERRY LEMONADE

Life's sweetest lemon found me in October. Ripe in the right places.
Tart and smart with his wit. Summer in his smirk. I collect the ways he
made me feel like they were mine. I take notes of the great butterfly
migration that scattered for him. He made me a hunter for the things I
cannot catch myself. He made me fear the feelings I used to hoard.

> (There has to be a riddle in the way I
>
> Cower at love while also crave for it
>
> To plague me.)

I remember squeezing for conversation until it was enough. I've
been parched under the same promise twice now, but he resembles
the faith I keep close. That love is as attainable as life allows it to
be. I wish I weren't my limitations, but this I can be patient for. I'm
hell-bent on finding my heaven-sent, but there is no grace in trying
to fill a lonely space. I am still sipping lemonade from life's sweetest
loves. Pink and strawberry kisses. There will be more sour faces. More
lessons to pulp. I am not done squeezing the hell out of love's skin.

(SISTER'S ADVICE)

Winter strips me of these dead leaves,
And the wind still shakes the limbs.

But bare doesn't always mean broken.

LUX

You noticed me that one time
And I have it saved.
I still have that sticker you like.
I don't know your name but I would like to.
Hell, I would die to figure it out. They would
Lay me in the coffin, smirk up, if I knew.
And we are at the same place again.
Same burnt-coffee fragrance, same nervous sighs.
Do you see me looking, babe?
Do you see my invisible gestures calling you closer?
They close at ten, but I won't panic for contact.
I'll see you next time.

Will I ever gain the strength in my throat to voice
This ringer of want? An alarm always going off.
Kiss me hard at first to snooze me
Then do it once more, but slowly.
Don't lose me if you don't have to;
Don't forget my crossed legs and
The poems I write for you.
May you read them next spring,
May they be available in print.
Remember my clumsy hands the best you can.
Mark my attempts absent,
I'll shoot my shot soon,
I've been practicing.

I WILL FIND SOMEONE
IN THIS LIFETIME
THAT GIVES ME
THE SAME KIND
OF WILD WONDERFUL
YOU GAVE ME

I THINK HER NAME WAS EMMA

I once saw a girl
At the meet-and-greet
Who looked just like you.
A doe, she was so pretty.

Made me question what I'm attracted to.
I found that love is fluid if you just feel it through.

Desire and craving bind the bones that ache
In my hands to hold another's face.

Though the more I open up, the more my bluff
Does not match the heart on my sleeve.
If I just go with the flow, I know fate will interject.

STUDIO

Alone is a roommate
I share a bed with.
They are cozy and
They know me, but even
Meteors crash when
They are tired of the
Quiet, hurtling around
With their own weight.
It's no surprise when
They finally break and
Fall straight into the
Closest thing that will
Hold them in place.

LANDMARKS

I was taking note on how to love my company,

And you kept waiting for me to be something to save.

I'm not the thumb-drawn hitchhiker you wanted me to be.

I'm not the wild tornado begging for direction.

I know my footsteps' secrets, and they're my favorite to tell.

May you forever know the places you can no longer call out for me.

I won't dwell on my past,

About a love I thought would last.

I'll learn to let old love pass on to the great beyond.

THE Q

I ride the subway now and I'm going south,
But I still miss your mouth and my old house.
I studied the subway's nomenclature
Without spelling your name, and I sway in peace
Knowing nothing here leads back to you.

There's so much freedom in forgetting.

I am the greatest love
I have ever known.

HYPOCRITICAL

I don't review the previous years I've lived
And people I've been as something cringe.
All the expired versions of myself loved me
Then, so why would I regret existing
As someone I once loved being?

SUPERHUMAN

Life happened by chance and I never asked for it.
I could have been a million other things, and
Now I pay taxes and think and think and think.
It's a beautiful burden all in one. And I could
Live it, but I really try to love it. I'm here in this
Span and want to make a name out of who I am.
The characters I'll become will be heroes. Each one
Saving the last. And when I'm older, fists on hips,
I will know I have lived and lived and lived.

MEANTIME

Real life is not afraid to live without me,
And it I keep waiting for the wanting to
Finally give in, I may look back at all the
Lifetimes landfilled and wonder
What I would've done with the time
I spent loitering for love.

GREAT WHITE THING

There are gold mines past the shoreline,
I'm sure of it.
I used to be a tiny coral reef,
A small heartbeat in this big escape
But after the wind, I became
A great white thing.
All sharp teeth without bite.
Still holding fear in my gills.
           Still breathing it in.
I look the part: much bigger than
What are still the smallest parts of me.

I'll pull waves back in before they crash.
I'll watch my footing once I reach the shore.
I'll throw any graceless hands overboard.
I must try at least.

STILL,

My favorite part of becoming
Is reintroducing myself as the soul
Who made it through the black hole.
Who bought back the stars stolen
From the skies I dreamt on.
And darling, do I dream, still.

I dream so much bigger than anything I've ever done.
It's the most human part of my nature.

MOVING ALONE IN YOUR TWENTIES

I broke down to my folks after I shipped my shit
And moved across the country all alone.

Watched anxiety surface like lumps in my throat.
Shortened my vocabulary and used smaller words.
Found cracks in my speech when counting the names
Who gifted me this grief.

I've been tearing the paper and cutting the ribbons for years now,
Tired of unwrapping the same damn thing. I know what's inside.
Lately it's been hard to catch me by surprise.
It's always been hard to catch me at all.
I don't think better comes; I think it waits for me
To adjust my coming-of-age. The way a season breathes in
The arrival of change.

I'M CHASING THE SEASONS;
THEY'RE CHANGING FASTER THAN ME.
I DON'T KNOW WHO I'LL BE IN THE SPRING
BUT I'M GROWING THERE, SLOWLY.

SOMEWHERE GREAT

And when I don't know where to go from here,
Take what's left of me to the mountains.
I want to see the view before I go.
I want to sprinkle my apology into the wind.
I hope a migration catches it on their way.
I hope they drop it off at your front porch.
I hope you read it slow and it makes you say

"I'm sorry too."

I taught myself not to hand out forgiveness
To those who won't take responsibility first.
You rebuilt a wall in me that's four feet taller.
I can't see over it yet but I will.
I've heard it's beautiful,
But I'm lonely behind here.
I'm carving out a window with my painted nails.
I laugh. I see I still haven't given up on escapes.
I tell myself to wait and see.
I carry the silence with the lines in my hands,
And I don't need a reading.
I know I'm on my way to somewhere great.

FRUITION

Nothing has been properly ours to give it a name.
Nothing with a date of birth or territory to claim.
Maybe love is something always in fruition. I'm not positive.
Though it might be ripe, does it make it right? I'm not sure either.
You don't have to answer. Though I know you never do.

    I visit the market without you.
    Buy blueberry muffins but take the blueberries out.
    I'm sure there's a metaphor in there.
    How I crave the very thing I take out.
    Avoid the texture. Run from the way it feels,
    Even when I know it could be sweet.

YOU CAN STILL BE GROWING EVEN IF IT FEELS LIKE WITHERING.

EVEN WHEN THE DAYS FEEL PARCHED AND SUN-DRIED.

GROWTH DOESN'T ALWAYS HAVE TO FEEL COMFORTABLE.

GROWTH ISN'T ALWAYS GOING TO FEEL LIKE GROWING.

THE WAY

I look at the dirt on my feet.
I study the footprints I've made
And how far they've taken me.

But I don't dare ignore the steps I've taken back.
The ones I have reclaimed
And the ones I'm too scared to name.

Even all my mistakes and regrets
Have taken me to where
I'm meant to go next.

ACRES

It's April again, and I forget how grief never misses an anniversary.
It blooms like the boy who visits my state but never calls my name.
It bends like my grandmother's knees when she fell the first time.
It grows like the fears I never even knew I could be afraid of.
It spreads like dreams that fell out of the skies I wished on.

      I should own land for all this loss.

Last spring I stripped my skeleton, stored bad bones in the closet.
You could assemble them now and they might make up
Half the man that once looked like me. So I built sacred cemeteries.
Lonely acres that had room to heal, and I am healing.
These gardens know grief, but they are abundant like me.
They are rooted in resilience, and so am I.

WORTHY

Maybe I am the bad guy in my dreams.

Maybe I am the monster who crawls out

From under the bed just to tuck myself in.

Maybe my love is just as cruel in my fantasies

As it is in my reality.

Maybe I am not the villain nor the hero

But the city they burned.

Still recovering.

Still worth rebuilding.

RESTORATION

I seem to chase memory
Like dogs chase the days.
Reminisce on who I've missed
And the confidants who stayed.
I could be the beautiful boy in the galleries,
Wander like my head is on straight.
Look poised and preoccupied.
Detached from the lens of the male gaze.

I tightrope toward the Dutch masters.
Their still life. Their suspended presence.
How I used to be the *Girl with a Pearl Earring,*
Always looking back.

I am restoring damaged parts of myself
With fresh paint and varnish finish.
I'll be the most curious exhibit to visit.
Hung in wonderment.

WHAT WOUNDS ARE YOU SCRATCHING AT?

HOW WILL YOU SOOTHE THE ITCH?

I am brimming with gratitude for those who have brought this book to life.

Thank you to those who read and keep reading. Those who have watched my voice get louder. Thank you for listening.

Thank you to the inspiring team at Central Avenue Publishing. Michelle, Jessica, and Molly — it is a pleasure to learn from you all. Your spirit and guidance has carried me as an evolving writer. Thank you for paying attention.

Thank you to the hands that bruised mine. While I wish you flat tires and spam calls and every minor inconvenience, I can't help but be grateful for pulling these poems out of me.

Until next time,

— Zane Frederick

Zane Frederick resides in his hometown of Phoenix, Arizona, and has been navigating his way through his twenties and winging it. His newest collection, *Itch*, consists of two years' worth of grief, resentment, forgiveness, and self-reflection. These poems were a way for him to fully heal from the wounds that remained open. Zane is still writing and cautiously experiencing while making the most of his youth.

Catch up with him at @zanefrederickwrites.